AN

ADDRESS

DELIVERED AT

THE CONSECRATION OF EVERGREEN CEMETERY,

BRIGHTON,

WEDNESDAY, AUGUST 7, 1850.

BY FREDERIC A. WHITNEY,

MINISTER OF THE FIRST CHURCH.

With an Appendix.

BOSTON:

PRINTED BY JOHN WILSON,

21, School Street.

1850.

AN

ADDRESS

DELIVERED AT

THE CONSECRATION OF EVERGREEN CEMETERY,

BRIGHTON,

WEDNESDAY, AUGUST 7, 1850.

BY FREDERIC A. WHITNEY,

MINISTER OF THE FIRST CHURCH.

With an Appendix.

BOSTON:
PRINTED BY JOHN WILSON,
21, SCHOOL STREET.
1850.

"With thy rude ploughshare, Death, turn up the sod,
And spread the furrow for the seed we sow:
This is the field and acre of our God;
This is the place where human harvests grow!"

LONGFELLOW.

ADDRESS.

The sacred hymns which have now resounded through these groves, the words of Scripture, and the voice of prayer, have all denoted the purpose for which we have gathered. We are drawn hither to-day by the promptings of our nature, and by the hopeful assurances of Christian faith, to set apart this place by appropriate services for the burial of the dead. It seems well designed for the object to which it is henceforth devoted. The progress of settlements seems for this to have spared the wide, well-wooded tract. The pleasant singing of the birds, and the gentle whispering of the boughs, as they are swayed in the summer wind, seem inviting and welcoming us to come and choose here the peaceful resting-place for our beloved and for ourselves. And, yielding to all these kindly calls, we have come, — childhood, that so wonders at the grave; youth and manhood and age, since all through the grave must pass. We have come to mark by religious rites the opening of this place, which waits the hand of art and taste to become, ere long, a garden of graves; and which waits, in the sorrows of bereavement, in the sympathies of affection, in the heavenward thoughts and hopes of the moved heart, a tenderer, a perpetual consecration.

By recent purchase, this ample enclosure, so long connected with an honored estate, has become the property of the town, in its corporate capacity to be held sacred to this one purpose for ever. The purchase and the purpose remind us of that touching narrative of the ancient Scripture, wherein Abraham buys of the children of Heth a burial-place for his dead. Sir William Blackstone cites this incident in the life of the patriarch as the oldest purchase of land, according to the customs of commercial days, in the annals of the human race. Should not this striking coincidence for ever admonish mankind how inseparably associated is the grave with all earthly possessions? Among the nations of the past in early times, it was held disreputable that one should be buried, save from necessity, in another's ground and tomb. And the aged patriarch declines the generous offer of the children of Heth, conveyed in terms of surpassing tenderness: "In the choice of our sepulchres bury thy dead: none of us shall withhold his sepulchre, but that thou mayest bury thy dead;" — and, by the equitable payment of silver, "current money with the merchant," says the venerable narrative, makes sure unto himself "the field of Ephron and the cave which was therein, and all the trees that were in the field, that were in all the borders round about, for a possession of a burying-place." The transaction indicates that regard for the final rest of the mortal body which seems native to the soul, so universally has it been manifested; and which, through the lapse of almost four thousand years, is still discerned, in that morning twilight of history, as a mild star among less interesting details.

The best sentiments of the heart have prompted man in all ages to provide carefully and affectionately for the remains of the dead. "Places of Repose," "Cities of the Silent," "Fields of Peace," "Cities of the Dead," — by these, and by names alike well chosen, have the places of interment been designated in ancient times. This disposal of the dead, ever a grateful and instructive, though a solemn and trying office, devolves upon the living. Neither nature, reason, nor scripture, seem to have determined beyond all human variance the most acceptable method and circumstances of this disposal. It has differed accordingly, history and experience tell us, with the progress of reason and philosophy, — with the unrelenting dictates of superstition, and with ever-varying taste. The methods of disposing of the dead which have obtained in different ages, and among the various tribes and nations, constitute a most interesting portion of the history of the race. The subject, both in ancient and modern time, has attracted the attention of the curious, who have furnished full and most engaging results, important alike for their bearings on the condition and progress of man as a being related to a life beyond the grave, on the advancement of science, and on the truth of religion. Into so wide a field does the subject open, that it must obviously be passed by here. We may observe only, that the prevailing customs have fallen, for the most part, under three classes, — embalming, burning, and burial in the earth; and that each evinces a common interest in the final disposal of the mortal dust. Each assures us, that the human body, that with which so mysteriously the undying soul has been connected, and through which alone it has been manifested, has been always invested with peculiar interest when the soul has parted from it. And whether embalmed for preservation through ages, as with the Egyptians, — whether reduced to its kindred ashes by the bright flames, those ashes meanwhile carefully preserved in golden urns or cherished mausoleums, as in the early days of Greece, and of which Homer so fully informs us, among the Romans and the northern tribes of Europe; or whether committed to the bosom of its native earth by burial, as was the earliest, and we must feel the most grateful, method of disposing of the body, — the body, nevertheless, clothed in the still majesty of death, has been henceforth sacred, and the spot where it rests has become hallowed ground.

We discharge, then, a natural service in these rites to-day. And the office which the truest affection and sympathies of the heart thus prompt is not less imperatively demanded by the wants of our town here in the immediate suburbs of a great city, and by the sure and rapid inroads of mortality. We hardly realize, amidst the busy scenes of life, how fast the silent halls of death are peopled. Let this be considered, and none, I think, will deem this place, devoted now to the dead, at all too spacious for our needs. We forget how soon, unless the amplest provision be made, each narrow bed in the enclosure we set apart, and hallow by our warmest love and truest prayers and worthiest tears, will be filled with its dreamless sleeper. Comparing several independent series of observations on human mortality, we infer that the entire population of the earth dies in about thirty-three years. We may estimate that population now at about ten hundred millions. How impressive becomes the statement, yet all reliable, that, in the short space of thirty-three years, ten hundred millions more will have been committed to the bosom of the earth! Each hour that revolves so soon tolls to their burial between three and four thousand of our race. Each second, that flies with the single breath we draw, tells that one human being more has yielded up the spirit to God who gave it, the mortal dust to the earth as it was. And further, — when we are assured by travellers of the immense catacombs of Egypt, which, though extending miles, have been crowded with the remains of the departed; when we consider how inadequate throughout the old world is the provision made for the dead, especially in and about the most populous cities; nay, when we look through our own land, at the single commercial city of New Orleans, for instance, and reflect how the busy tide of enterprise has hardly left among the thick habitations of men a single quiet spot for the dead, we are most convinced of the necessity of meeting early and supplying generously this urgent want of our common humanity.

I believe we feel the necessity of making this provision now to answer the wants of our own town. We cannot but rejoice in the general unanimity with which the proposal to procure a spacious and retired cemetery has been received. Nor can we forget the good spirit with which individual preferences, which might have led some of our citizens to another selection, have been yielded for the general choice. To the gentlemen of the Committee, who have devised and superintended the enterprise, and who present us to-day with a result so satisfactory of their taste and care and diligence, our warmest acknowledgments are gratefully rendered. And on us, as citizens of the town, receiving at their hand the work they have so auspiciously commenced, the rites of this consecration hour impose an obligation, I trust we shall willingly discharge, to carry out successfully the noble undertaking. We needed the place; and where, on the whole, could our want have been so well supplied? Where, with equal accommodation and satisfaction, could we have laid down our dead as in this peaceful retreat, near enough to the busy habitations of men, yet so retired as best to secure the happiest influences of such a spot? Where, on the whole, could the mourner have come with more tranquillity than here? Beneath what scenes of nature could the sorrowing heart have been more soothed than in these

> "Forests deep and lone,
> Where twilight shades are ever thrown,
> And murmuring winds with solemn tone
> Go slowly by,
> Sending a peal like ocean's moan
> Along the sky"?

I speak of a necessity. The little graveyard where we have been wont to go, early set apart on this side of the river by your fathers, who, though still connected with the ancient town of Cambridge, chose here to worship and here to bury their dead, has ceased to furnish accommodations for further interments. It was selected when as yet the busy sounds of labor and enterprise were little heard on its borders, and few habitations had grown up about it. It was laid near to the ancient house of worship; and the later church, which succeeded that time-worn edifice, went nearer towards it, as if linking in closer union the silent dead with the weekly prayers of the living for comfort and sanctification; its steeple looking down upon the graves, and realizing in a measure the beautiful sentiment of the poet: —

"The dead in Christ they rest in hope,
And o'er their sleep sublime
The shadow of the steeple moves
From morn to vesper chime.
On every mound in solemn shade
Its imaged form doth lie,
As goes the sunlight to the west,
Or rides the moon on high."

The small and sparse population which, a century since, was accustomed to worship here, and to whom doubtless the spot chosen for the dead seemed ample, has been succeeded by a comparatively large and thriving town. The years which have thus gone silently have yet gathered within those narrow limits many a loved and cherished form. Three or four generations have already mingled their dust in that hallowed ground. And while, from necessity, we are led to set apart this ampler place, which, in turn, shall be hallowed by dear and sacred memories, we cannot but bestow our benediction anew on those thick green graves, and hear the voice which breathes from the spot so long trod by the bereaved, and so peopled with the dead. We would consecrate this chosen place, in part, by fond remembrances of that we leave.

"Go where the ancient pathway guides,
See where our sires laid down
Their smiling babes, their cherished brides,
The patriarchs of the town:
Hast thou a tear for buried love?
A sigh for transient power?
All that a century left above, —
Go, read it in an hour."

There blends the unconscious dust of how great a company, — of beautiful children, of young men and maidens, of fathers and mothers, who, with the changing seasons of successive years, were borne out from the circles of usefulness and affection to the silent grave! What words of counsel, warning, and reproof, — what heavenly themes of consolation and hope mingle, if we listen aright, in the breeze that stirs those grassy mounds! How impressively do those early and later graves speak to us, engaged in this grateful service, of the change of all things earthly! How fruitful in the best lessons on human life and destiny! How do they plead with us for virtue and holiness, as with such as are yet strangers and sojourners on the earth!

And now, as with these voices falling on our ears, we are henceforth to weave about this place holy associations and cherished memories. We consecrate it to the repose of the dead, by beautifying these grounds, and rendering them in their outward aspect ever more attractive to the living. We would not only provide ample space for the undisturbed repose of the departed, but we would remove, so far as we may, the reproach, which, often justly, I fear, has rested on New England, that her burying-grounds have been her most forsaken, her most neglected enclosures. Consecrated to the rest and memory of the dead, we would make the spot most pleasing and instructive to the living.

We find encouragement to this in the good spirit which, within a few years, has prevailed in regard to our burying-places. Pere la Chaise, Paris, 1804, was the first modern cemetery laid out and ornamented as a public burying-place. Mount Auburn, in this country, followed in 1831. Greenwood Cemetery at Brooklyn, and Mount Hope at Rochester, N. Y.; Laurel Hill at Philadelphia; Harmony Grove at Salem; Forest Hills here on our right at Roxbury; Oak Hill at Newburyport; and pleasant rural cemeteries at Springfield, Lowell, Worcester, Framingham, Plymouth, Chelsea, and in various other places, — all tell of an improving taste in this respect.

But, though public attention has been much directed to the subject of adorning these sacred spots, still to some it may yet appear a superfluous work. A work not quite in keeping with the essential elements of the New England character, some may hold this of devising and maintaining a garden of graves. While I glory in the New England name, I do not forget that the pious fathers of New England, as the historian of the United States writes of them so sententiously, would have dug no graves in consecrated ground, and would bury their dead without a prayer. Should they look on us with the same eyes with which they looked their last on earth, our grateful service to-day, I fear, they would count an offence. Indeed, have not their descendants — we, the New England people — studied rather how best we should order our affairs for the purpose of living, than how our mortal remains should be disposed of when we were dead?

Thus in part, perhaps, it has happened, that, with recent exceptions, the external appearance of our New England burying-grounds has been uninviting to the eye; and so have they been uninstructive, unfrequented by our people, save when bearing in their dead. They have seldom been places of habitual resort, where encouraging moral and religious reflections might be awakened. Few had connected with them pleasant associations. Few had entered there to hear instructive voices whispering better things than of earth, from the spiritual world, whither this silent people had gone. Unconsecrate they have too often been, not in form alone, but in reality; and their holy lessons all unheeded in the desolation that brooded over them.

Because, as we believe, the best dictates of the heart and the teachings of Christianity forbid this; because, as we cannot forget, the Saviour was laid in a garden, in that new sepulchre which was hewn out of the rock, we would consecrate this place by allying with its natural charms the attractions of art and taste and affection. Not for the advantage of the dead, we know, shall be made these adornments, but for the living. Their poor dust, we know, as it shall mingle here with the earth, can be no longer blessed by our kindness or care. But that we may keep our own affections warm, and the memory of our friends ever green, we would devote this place henceforth to those kindly offices of affection which shall render it most inviting and edifying to the living. We consecrate it thus to the familiar intercourse of kindred and friends with the departed, and to the grateful musings of the thoughtful and devout. Through the happy influence of these peaceful and well-ordered shades, blending with the teachings of Christian faith, we would have the departed regarded, not as "lost, but as gone before;" not as widely severed from the living, but as treasures laid up on high. The biographer of the Earl of Ormond relates of him, that, when condoled with on the death of his son Lord Ossory, he nobly replied that "he would not exchange his dead son for any living one in Christendom." And even so may our burying-places, attracting the living to familiar communion with the departed, make real to faith and affection these invisible ones, and point us, as angel-messengers, to the future world.

> "When by a good man's grave I muse alone,
> Methinks an angel sits upon the stone:
> Like those of old on that thrice-hallowed night,
> Who sat and watched in raiment heavenly bright;
> And, with a voice inspiring joy and fear,
> Says, pointing upward, that he is not here;
> That he is risen."

To the Christian teachings of immortality, to the blessed hopes with which the Saviour has lighted the chambers of death, be this spot for ever consecrated. The place where our kindred and friends shall lie, and we ourselves may be laid, — be it henceforth associated in our minds but with cheerful, hopeful remembrances and anticipations. Let the beaten and pleasant paths run along among the silent mansions of the dead. Let them be studded with trees, mingling in every season their varied foliage. Let these groves be the undisturbed resort of the birds; singing, early and late, morning notes of triumph, as for the risen spirit; gentler evening dirges, as for sorrowing affection. Let flowers adorn these borders, emblems of perennial verdure in the better land; so that the young shall not shun these places in their evening walks, and the old shall turn hither with tranquil satisfaction, and the traveller stop awhile to rest, as they whose forms lie beneath him are resting at the end of their earthly journey. Let the spot invite thither, like a garden, the bereaved, for solace and meditation and heavenly communion; and consecrate it shall indeed become, as with immortal hopes, inspired of him who died for us and rose again, and spoiled the grave of its victory.

The grave, — the grave, — to all which that word involves of counsel and admonition, of hope and peace, we consecrate this place. To salutary lessons on the end of human life be it devoted. Of the supreme importance of using life as a precious opportunity, a holy trust for which we are accountable to

God, be these whispering groves, be the storied monuments and engraven stones, as they shall presently stand here in solemn silence, impressive preachers to us all! Here, in peace, may we commune with the spirit-land. Here may the distant world be brought near to human thought. Here may earthliness and pride and passion be put utterly away. Here, in the multitude of their thoughts within them, may the afflicted be comforted and edified. Here, as the mourner comes to weep apart, may it be with that sacred grief that shall keep the lost on earth in hopeful and perpetual fellowship. Be it that grief, "invoking him to peace," which Campbell denotes so well in his "Theodric," when he sings of one bereaved, who,

> "Though he mourned her long, 'twas with such woe,
> As if her spirit watched with him below."

Soon the grave will offer here its holy counsels. Soon to its quiet chambers will be borne in here the bodies of the departed. Not by man's ordering, but by the divine appointment, will these vacant lots be one by one inhabited by the dead. Nor can we, therefore, doubt the wisdom and benignity of the appointment, whether it shall people them with the aged, weary, and oppressed, whose spirits, as lone angels, seem beckoned upward by their generation departed, or with the young of brightest promise. The Grecian historian tells us of the Athenians, that they were wont to bury the young before the rays of the morning had begun to gild the earth, that the glorious sun might not look on decay so premature.

A better faith than the Grecian enjoyed will help us to bring here even the young and useful, and yield them up in serene trust, as at the fit hour and no untimely offering, seeing that the Father hath need of them. All in God's good time shall come.

> "Here shall the weary rest,
> And souls, with woes oppressed,
> No more shall weep;
> And youth and age shall come,
> And beauty in her bloom,
> And manhood to the tomb,—
> Sweet be their sleep!"

To the spiritual world, through the portals of the tomb, we all are tending fast. As the funeral procession shall cross the threshold of these gates, may the words of Scripture, which shortly are to be engraved above them, pour down celestial light, as heavenly stars, on the mourner's clouded way. May the name, by which henceforth this place is to be known, be significant alike of the memory ever green of the departed, and of the freshness of those Christian hopes which flourish even by the tomb.

"EVERGREEN CEMETERY,"—by our prayers and hymns, by the words we have uttered, and by the unspoken thoughts of this congregation, we consecrate it. By all the lessons and influences of the place,—by the tender charities of the human heart, and by the grace of God,—by the tears and loves and fond remembrances which it shall presently witness, we consecrate it, as with holiest baptismal vows, a quiet sanctuary for ever for the dead.

Within this circling grove where we are assembled

to-day, it is contemplated that a chapel may be erected, in which the last services over our dead, grateful alike to Christian faith and to bereaved affection, may be discharged. Thus happily the spot on which we are gathered for these opening rites may be the same on which, through coming years, the stricken mourner, kindred, and friends, will bow in prayer, before the forms of the beloved go down to their kindred dust. More and more consecrate be the place by each funereal train that winds through these paths, long after we have gone; by each prayer uttered or unspoken here; by each voiceless one, who, through these shades, shall go to swell the host of the dead!

And may Almighty God our Father, to whose protecting care we devote and commend these grounds in parting, bring us all at length to that world where sorrow and separation are unknown, and joy is eternal, through his infinite mercy in Jesus Christ our Lord! *Amen.*

APPENDIX.

Brighton was set off from Cambridge and incorporated, Feb. 28, 1807. The Charles River divides the two places. The first Meeting-house was built here in 1744; though, several years earlier, the inhabitants worshipped in a private house, while yet connected with the Old Cambridge Church. The ancient volume of our Church-records is entitled, "The Records of the Third Church of Christ in Cambridge."

The only burying-place of which we know, was the one now in use on Market-street, which was purchased in 1764. Previously, those dying here were interred in the ancient Cambridge ground. Settlements were begun at Cambridge in 1631. The town-records, Jan. 4, 1635, speak first of the burying-ground thus: "It is further ordered that the Burying-place shall be paled in; whereof John Taylcot is to do 2 Rod, George Steele 3 Rod & a Gate, Thomas Hosmer 3 Rod, Mathew Allen 1 Rod, & Andrew Warner appointed to get the remainder done at a publick charge & he is to have iii. s. a Rod."

In 1845, Mr. William T. Harris, of Cambridge, then student of Harvard University, transcribed the epitaphs in the Old Cambridge burying-ground. They were very neatly published in a small volume, which, as it contains the names of many of the early settlers of this place, then the south end of Cambridge, will be found interesting to our citizens. Among the epitaphs and monumental inscriptions, we read the names of Brown, Champney, Cheney, Clark, Coolidge, Dana, Ellis, Fessenden, Foster, Gardner, Hastings, Hill, Jackson, Learnard, Livermore, Oldham, Oliver, Phipps, Robbins, Smith, Sparhawk, Thwing, Warren, White, Winship, all of which were names of residents on this side; and of others, many, who, before their marriage, bore the names of residents here.

The inhabitants on this side of the river, finding it inconvenient to go to that first burying-ground, provided one here, as we have seen, in 1764, and as appears by the ancient Deed; a copy of which we present from the original, preserving the old orthography and punctuation:—

Know all men by these presents that I Nathaniel Sparhawke of Cambridge in the County of Middlesex in the Province of the Massachusetts Bay in New England; Yeoman; for & in consideration of the Sum of thirteen pounds Six Shillings and Eight pence Lawfl: money paid me by a Certain Number of the Inhabitants of the first Precinct in Cambridge aforesd: who Dwell upon the South Side of Charles River (whose Names are hereafter annexed) the Receipt whereof I do Acknowledge; Do hereby Give, Grant & Convey to the Inhabitants aforesd: half an Acre of Land in Cambridge aforesd: Bounded Westerly on a Town way there Measuring Eight Rods & four feet; Northerly; Easterly; & Southerly; on the sd: Nathaniel Sparhawke's Land; the Dividing line beginning ad a Stake and Heap of Stones by ye Way aforesd: & Runing Easterly Nine Rods and five feet to a Stake & Stones about it; and from thence Runing Southerly Eight Rods to an other Stake with Stones about it; & from thence Runing Westerly Ten Rods & two third parts of a Rod to a Stake & Stones about it ad Sd: Way; which Stake & Stones is Eight Rods & four feet Southerly of ye Stake & Stones first Mentioned; To Have and To Hold; the same to such of the Inhabitants of the first Precinct in Cambridge as shall Dwell upon the Southerly side of Charles River as aforesd: forever; To & for the Use following; Namely; for a place Wherein to bury Such of the Inhabitants & others that may Die in that part of the first Precinct in Cambridge which lies Southerly of Charles River as aforesd: The Partition Fences between ye half acre of Land aforesd: and the Land adjoining thereunto; to be forever hereafter made & maintained by such of the Inhabitants of the Parish aforesd: as live on the Southerly Side of Charles River as aforesd: and I do hereby bind myself & my Heirs to Warrant and Defend the half Acre of Land aforesd: to ye Sd: Grantees against the Lawfull Claims and Demands of all Persons; so long as the same Land is or shall be Used and improved for the purpose aforesd: and the Partition fences aforesd: are Made and Maintained as aforesd: In Witness whereof I together with Lydia my Wife in Token of her Consent hereunto and the Relinquishment of her Right of Dower in the aforegranted Premises; Have hereunto Sett our Hands & Seals: this fifth Day of March in the fourth year of the Reign of King George ye third — Annoque Domini 1764:

Signed Sealed & Delivered
in presence of us —
Eben Sparhawke
Nathan Sparhawk

Nathel. Sparhawke
Lydia Sparhawke.

Middlesex S.S May 15th: AD 1765
the above Named Nathaniel Sparhawke & Lydia Sparhawke freely acknowledged the foregoing Instrument to be their Voluntary Act and Deed before me Thos: Greenwood, Justice of Peace

This Deed given to Thomas Sparhawke, William Dana and Samuel Phipps in behalf of the Subscribers.

Middlesex Ss 19th Novemr 1805.
Received & entered in the Registry of deeds, book 165 page 294
Attest Saml Bartlett, Regr:

Mr. Nathaniel Sparhawke, who conveyed this land, was father of Mr. Edward Sparhawk now resident with us in remarkable vigor, having nearly attained his eightieth year, and who owns, and, with his son Edward Corey Sparhawk, occupies the estate at the corner of Washington and Cambridge Streets, which was owned and occupied by his father, and by four generations in lineal succession before him. Thus seven generations have occupied the place. The estate originally extended from Washington-street to Charles River; and it was bounded west by the Richard Dana Estate, on a line where now runs Market-street. The family is perhaps the most ancient among us. Nathaniel (1) its progenitor came from England with his family early, and was admitted Freeman in 1639. He was Representative from 1642 to 1647, and died June 28, 1647. His son Nathaniel (2) married, 31st October, 1649, Patience, daughter of Rev. Sam Newman, of Rehoboth. His son Nathaniel (3) was Deacon of the Cambridge Church (as was the first Nathaniel), and died Nov. 8, 1734, aged 67 years and 10 days (see Harris's Epitaphs). He had a son Nathaniel (4), of Harvard University, 1715; and also a son Noah, who died Feb. 4, 174$\frac{8}{9}$, aged 51 years, 11 months, and 20 days (see Harris's Epitaphs). The oldest child of Noah was Nathaniel, who sold the burying-ground, whose stone stands there and tells that he was born Oct. 28, 1727, and died Oct. 1, 1777. Eleven of the family have graduated at Harvard University, and six of the name at Dartmouth College.

Eben and Nathan Sparhawk, witnesses to the Deed, were brothers of Nathaniel the signer. Eben graduated at Harvard University in 1756, was settled in 1761 second minister of Templeton, and died in 1805. Nathan was Colonel of the Militia; lived and died at Barre. Thomas Sparhawke named at the foot of the Deed, was cousin of Nathaniel, and occupied the place on Faneuil-street, now occupied by

George H. Brooks. The slab over his tomb in our ground is thus inscribed: " Intombed — Thomas Sparhawke Esq. who died Augt. 15th 1785 Æts. 77." William Dana, named in connection, was of the ancient Dana family; and Samuel Phipps was of an early family here, whose estate was that on the south-west corner of Washington and Allston Streets, afterwards the Livermore Place.

The burying-ground was formerly entered through a common wooden gate. The iron gates and granite posts were erected about twelve years since; and the wall on Market-street, about twenty years before.

In the warrant for the annual March meeting of 1846, was this article: " To see if the town will take measures for enlarging the old or providing a new burying-ground;" and the subject was committed to Messrs. Henry H. Learnard, Edward Sparhawk, and Samuel Brooks, to report thereon subsequently. No report appears to have been presented; and, in March 1848, the subject was committed to the same gentlemen, who reported, June 19, several tracts of land, which they had examined, suitable for the purpose, together with the prices affixed. Whereupon, they were instructed by the town to purchase such a lot as they might think advisable. Messrs. Benjamin F. Peirce and Willard H. Giles were added to the Committee.

This Committee reported, Nov. 20, the selection and purchase of the " Aspinwall Woods," a tract of nearly 14 acres, lying on South-street, at $300 per acre; being about half the price per acre of either of the other lots offered. Whereupon, the Treasurer was authorized to give notes in behalf of the town for the payment of the same. Messrs. N. Martin, C. Spring, W. C. Allen, J. M. Whittemore, and E. Chamberlin, were chosen a Committee to procure an accurate survey of the grounds, and to report a plan for laying them out. They engaged the services of Mr. Wm. A. Mason, Civil Engineer, of Cambridge, and on the 6th of January submitted to the town a plan, which was adopted. The Selectmen, William R. Champney, Reuben Hunting, and John Gordon, together with Messrs. T. Munroe, E. Chamberlin, J. M. Whittemore, C. Spring, and F. L. Winship, were appointed a Committee to prepare the grounds according to the same.

On the 13th of January, Mr. Augustus Aspinwall, in behalf of the heirs of the late William Aspinwall, acknowledged the receipt from the Treasurer of $4023.75 for the ground, as containing thirteen acres one quarter and twenty-six rods. On the Committee's subsequent survey, it was found that the ground embraced nearly fourteen acres.

Nov. 9. The Committee reported progress, and were instructed by the town to fix the price of lots at ten dollars for the present; and to offer at public auction, as soon as practicable, the right of choice to the same. — April 1. The Committee again reported to the town their doings and recommendations. — May 6. The Committee were instructed by the town to carry out their original design in all particulars, except that they erect on South-street a fence of wood, instead of iron, as first contemplated. This fence with the gateway having been erected, and the receiving tomb in North Grove built during the summer, the avenues and paths laid out and graded, Wednesday the 7th day of August, four o'clock, P.M. was assigned for the CONSECRATION OF THE CEMETERY.

Notice of the consecration was published in the "Boston Transcript," the "Christian Register," and "Christian Inquirer" of August 3d, and in other Boston papers of the 5th and 6th.

Seats were arranged in Chapel Grove, a spacious and beautifully wooded grove of circular shape, ten rods in diameter, reserved for the future erection of a chapel, exactly in the centre of the grounds. A large audience was seated facing the south. A platform was erected for the speakers near the southern boundary, on which were seated likewise several of the aged men of the town. The band and the choir of singers had places on either side of the platform. The following was the Order of Services at the Consecration: —

I. INSTRUMENTAL MUSIC. BY THE BAND.

II. HYMN. BY REV. JAMES FLINT, D.D.

From thee, O God! our spirits come,
  Enshrined in breathing clay;
Mysterious guests! not here at home,
  Nor destined long to stay.

Be these sequestered haunts of mound,
  And slope of dell and glade,
Approached henceforth as hallowed ground,
  Where life's pale wrecks are laid!

Oh! why then mourn that earth to earth
  And dust to dust is given?
'Tis but the spirit's second birth,
  Its coronal for heaven.

We yield the body to its doom,
  The dust in dust to lie;
Yet we may deem beside the tomb
  The spirit hovering nigh.

And oft our steps shall linger near,
  Till death the veil remove,
And kindred spirits sundered here
  Be joined in deathless love.

III. SELECTION FROM THE SCRIPTURES. BY REV. ARTHUR SWAZEY.

IV. PRAYER. BY REV. MR. SWAZEY.

V. HYMN. BY REV. CYRUS H. FAY.

When rose the Saviour from the tomb,
He robbed it of its deepest gloom,
Sealed hopeless grief's complaining lips,
And death became but life's eclipse.

Let hope, then, beam around the dead,
And faith her holy influence shed:
Where nature doth her charms disclose,
There give their cherished dust repose.

Calm woodland shade! we here would lay
The ashes of our loved away,
And come at length ourselves to sleep
Where thou wilt peaceful vigil keep.

And when around our graves shall bend,
In bitter grief, the faithful friend,
Oh! let thy peace sink on the soul,
And soothe it to thy sweet control!

VI. ADDRESS. BY REV. FREDERIC A. WHITNEY.

VII. HYMN. BY REV. JOHN PIERPONT.

To thee, O God! in humble trust,
Our hearts their cheerful incense burn
For this thy word, "Thou art of dust,
And unto dust shalt thou return."

For what were life, life's work all done,
The hopes, joys, loves, that cling to clay, —
All, all departed, one by one,
And yet life's load borne on for aye!

Decay! decay! 'tis stamped on all, —
All bloom in flower and flesh shall fade:
Ye whispering trees, when we shall fall,
Be our long sleep beneath your shade!

Here to thy bosom, mother earth,
Take back in peace what thou hast given;
And all that is of heavenly birth,
O God! in peace recall to heaven.

VIII. BENEDICTION.

Rev. Mr. Swazey, of the Second Church, offered a fervent and appropriate prayer, and read from the Scriptures the twenty-third chapter of Genesis, portions from the ninetieth Psalm, from the eleventh chapter of John, and from the fifteenth of the First Epistle to the Corinthians.

The singing was performed by ladies and gentlemen of Brighton, most of whom were at the time connected with the choirs of the churches, assisted by Miss Anna Stone, the distinguished vocalist, whose rare powers of voice have been well known and appreciated both at New York and Boston, and accompanied by the Roxbury Band. Should our notice of the interesting occasion fall a century hence under the eye of any of their descendants, it may be grateful to them to know, while meditating perhaps in these beautiful grounds among the graves of revered ancestors, that the voices of some among them joined in the hymns of praise which so helped to hallow the spot for the resting-place of those who sing no more on earth, but the songs of the Redeemed, it may be, above. We append, therefore, in alphabetical order, the names of those who, by their excellent service, contributed so largely to the interest and impressiveness of the occasion:

Messrs. Baxter, Daniel; Baldwin, Henry; Brackett, Albert; Breck, Joseph and Charles H. B.; Brewer, Alanson T.; Davis, Benj. D. of Brookline; Dearborn, Samuel; Giles, Willard H.; Hughan, Oscar; Pierce, Horace and Benj. F.; Roper, John; Ruggles, John; Stevens, Silas H.; Warren, George W. and John Q. A.; Wethern, Thomas; White, John.

Mrs. Brackett, Cephas H.; Ruggles, John. — Misses Dana, Catharine C.; Davis, Elizabeth A. of Brookline; Hollis, Mary L.; Hunting, Susanna; Kingsley, Frances S. and Sarah J.; Pierce, Sarah A. and Mary E.; Warren, Abby Ann and Adeliza; White, Nancy B.

The choice of lots in the Cemetery was offered at public auction, Monday afternoon succeeding the consecration; and sixty were taken at the appraised value, at sums for choice varying from twenty to five dollars. More have been taken since. A finely engraved plan of the Cemetery, prepared for the sale, shows the arrangement of the grounds, with the names of the groves, avenues, and paths. At a town meeting, held Aug. 19, Messrs. Wm. R. Champney, Ed. Chamberlin, and David Collins, were appointed Commissioners of the Cemetery. And we trust, that, under the regulations which shall be adopted for the ordering of the place, it will be daily becoming more pleasing to the eye of taste, as it grows more hallowed to memory and affection.

www.ingramcontent.com/pod-product-compliance
Lightning Source LLC
LaVergne TN
LVHW011140110826
845150LV00008B/2434
* 9 7 8 1 4 1 8 1 9 2 5 7 0 *